On the WING

North American Birds 5

Andrea Voon

Richard Han

Green-winged Teal

French: Sarcelle d'hiver

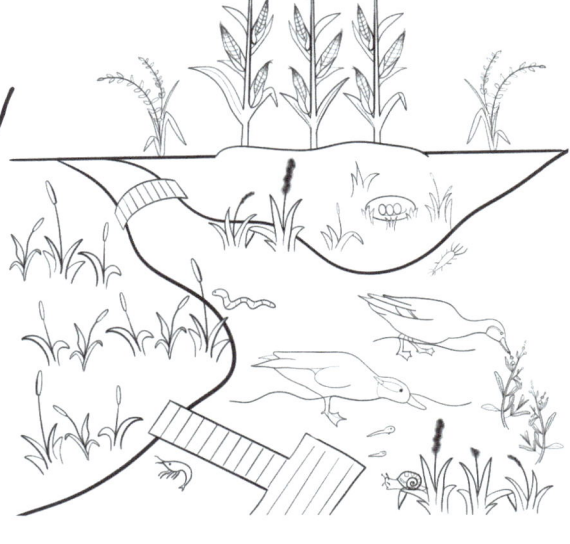

Great big wings, great big wings, flap flap flap...

Recycling agents in the marshes are on the wing.

Green-winged Teals, Green-winged Teals, clap clap clap...

Lift their wings and take-off straight in the spring.

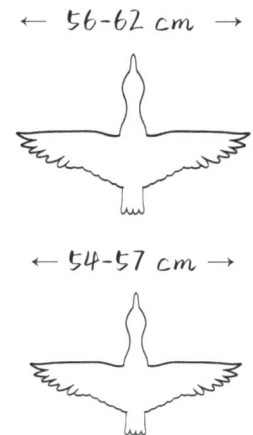

← 56–62 cm →

Blue-winged Teal

French: Sarcelle à ailes bleues

← 54–57 cm →

Cinnamon Teal

French: Sarcelle cannelle

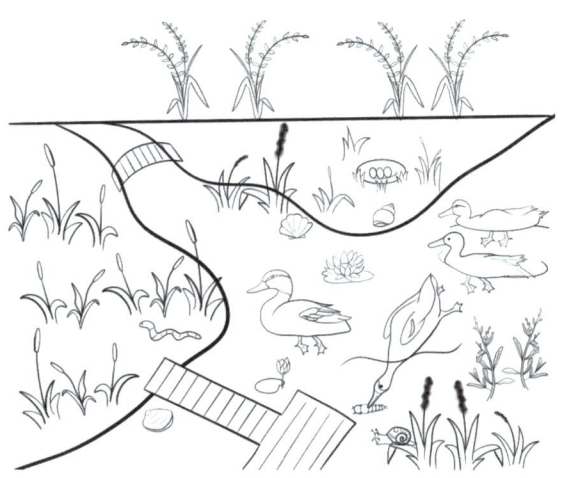

Great big wings, great big wings, flap flap flap…

Flight attendants in the marshes are on the wing.

Blue-winged Teals, Cinnamon Teals, clap clap clap…

Take-off early for migration in the spring.

← 62-63 cm →

Ring-necked Duck

French: Fuligule à collier

Great big wings, great big wings, flap flap flap...

Divers in the lakes and ponds are on the wing.

Ring-necked Ducks, Ring-necked Ducks, clap clap clap...

Leap and plunge underwater in the spring.

← 58-63 cm →

American Coot

French: Foulque d'Amérique

Great big wings, great big wings, flap flap flap…

Kung fu masters in the lakes and ponds are on the wing.

American Coots, American Coots, clap clap clap…

Run on water and muddy ground in the spring.

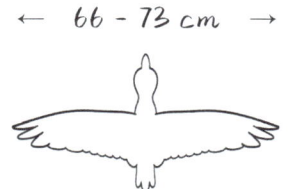

← 66 - 73 cm →

Wood Duck

French: Canard branchu

Great big wings, great big wings, flap flap flap...

Powwow dancers in the lakes and ponds are on the wing.

Wood Ducks, Wood Ducks, clap clap clap...

Perch and climb on tree branches in the spring.

Mandarin duck

French: Canard mandarin

← 65 – 75 cm →

Great big wings, great big wings, flap flap flap…

Chinese opera actors from East Asia are on the wing.

Mandarin Ducks, Mandarin Ducks, clap clap clap…

Raise their crest and show of "sail" feathers in the spring.

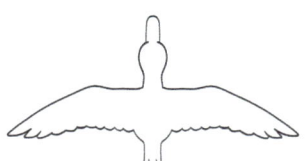

← 68 - 78 cm →

Lesser Scaup

French: Petit Fuligule

Great big wings, great big wings, flap flap flap…

Clam diggers in the lakes and ponds are on the wing.

Lesser Scaups, Lesser Scaups, clap clap clap…

Forage on the soft mud in the spring.

Common Goldeneye

French: Garrot à oeil d'or

← 77 - 83 cm →

Great big wings, great big wings, flap flap flap...

Opticians in the lakes and ponds are on the wing.

Common Goldeneyes, Common Goldeneyes, clap clap clap...

Perform a set of courtship moves in the spring.

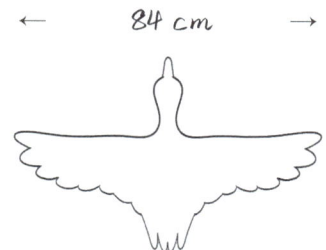

84 cm

Gadwall

French: Canard chipeau

Great big wings, great big wings, flap flap flap…

Tour guides in the marshes are on the wing.

Gadwalls, Gadwalls, clap clap clap…

Steal food from diving ducks in the spring.

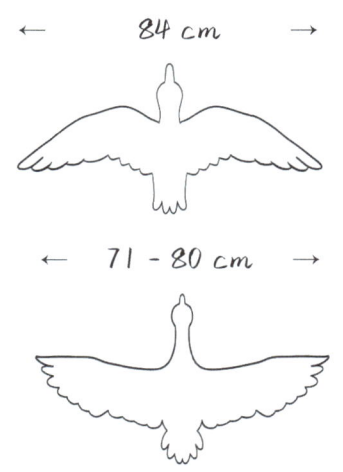

84 cm

71 - 80 cm

American Wigeon

French: Canard d'Amérique

Eurasian Wigeon

French: Canard siffleur

Great big wings, great big wings, flap flap flap…

Landscapers in the lakes and ponds are on the wing.

American Wigeons, Eurasian Wigeons, clap clap clap…

Pluck and nibble plants in the spring.

← 86.4 cm →

Northern Pintail

French: Canard pilet

Great big wings, great big wings, flap flap flap…

Teachers in the marshes are on the wing.

Northern Pintails, Northern Pintails, clap clap clap…

Dabble and swim with their pointy tail in the spring.

Tundra Swan

French: Cygne siffleur

168 cm

Great big wings, great big wings, flap flap flap...

Authors in the lakes and ponds are on the wing.

Mute Swans, Mute Swans, clap clap clap...

Raise their wing and sail elegantly in the spring.

Waterfowl, waterfowl, flap flap flap...

Find their perfect match on the wing.

Seasonal partners, lifelong partners, clap clap clap...

Prepare for the breeding season in the spring.

Author

Andrea Voon

Over the past few years, Andrea has learned and grown with her family as a full-time mother in Canada. Back in Malaysia, she was a Chinese immersion elementary school teacher. In 2021, Andrea started her journey as an author. Growing up in a multilingual environment, Andrea loves the beauty of languages on their own. She has the vision to publish picture books to support bilingual families in raising their children in English, Chinese, and Cantonese reading.

Photographer

Richard Han

Richard loves to practice patience through his lenses of the natural world. He enjoys observing the wildlife and photographing the natural lifestyles that animals live. He is excited to present the beautiful photos that he captured in dreamy tones and colors to all the birds lover.

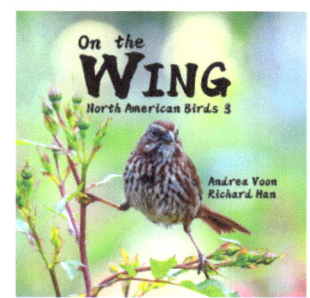

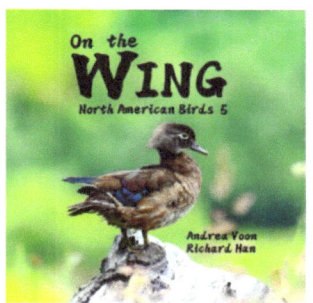

To **Shirley Han, Derek, Eliana, Alayna & Magnus Dominus**

with love -- Andrea. V

For **Richard Han**

The patience in natural photography

ISBN 978-1-998856-53-4
Text Copyright © 2024 Andrea Voon
Photo Credit © 2024 Richard Han